Journey to Freedom®

MATTHEW HENSON
AND THE NORTH POLE EXPEDITION

BY ANN GRAHAM GAINES

"MY THOUGHTS WERE ON THE
GOING AND GETTING FORWARD,
AND ON NOTHING ELSE."

~ MATTHEW HENSON ~

Cover and page 4 caption: Matthew Henson is dressed for an Arctic expedition.

Content Consultant:
Deirdre C. Stam
Associate Professor, Palmer
School of Library and
Information Science,
Long Island University

Author of the introduction
to Matthew A. Henson's
Historical Arctic Journey,
the explorer's autobiography

Published in the United States of America by The Child's World
1980 Lookout Drive, Mankato, MN 56003-1705
800-599-READ • www.childsworld.com

ACKNOWLEDGEMENTS

The Child's World: Mary Berendes, Publishing Director

The Design Lab: Kathleen Petelinsek, Design; Gregory Lindholm, Page Production

Red Line Editorial: Melissa Johnson, Editorial Direction

PHOTOS

Cover and page 4: Bettman/Corbis

Interior: Peary Macmillan Arctic Museum, Bowdoin College, 5, 10; The Design Lab, 7, 13; Photo Library, 8, 16, 17; Victor R. Boswell Jr./National Geographic/Getty Images, 9; Peter Harholdt/Corbis, 11; Library of Congress, 12, 14, 19, 20, 21, 23; Corbis, 18; Sissie Brimberg/National Geographic/Getty Images, 24; National Geographic/Getty Images, 25; Bettman/Corbis, 26, 27

LIBRARY OF CONGRESS CATALOGING-IN-PUBLICATION DATA

Gaines, Ann.

  Matthew Henson and the North Pole expedition / by Ann Graham Gaines.

    p. cm. — (Journey to freedom)

  Includes bibliographical references and index.

  ISBN 978-1-60253-130-7 (library bound : alk. paper)

  1. Henson, Matthew Alexander, 1866–1955—Juvenile literature. 2. African American explorers—Biography—Juvenile literature. 3. North Pole—Discovery and exploration—Juvenile literature. I. Title. II. Series.

  G635.H4.G35 2009

  910.92—dc22

  [B]

                                        2009003650

CONTENTS

Chapter One

PEARY AND HENSON

n 1908 and 1909, black explorer
Matthew Henson took part in a great
adventure. He went on an **expedition**
to the North Pole.

The leader of the expedition was a white man
named Robert Peary. For years, Peary had dreamed
of becoming the first person to reach the pole. He
and Henson had failed in several attempts. Peary
believed he had one last chance to explore the
Arctic. At nearly 53 years old, Peary no longer felt
as strong as he once did. He knew he must plan the
expedition carefully.

Peary found a group of brave, smart men to go
with him. They would leave solid land and cross
the ice-covered Arctic Ocean. They would travel so

far north, they would be the only humans for hundreds of miles. There would be no villages where the explorers could stop for rest or supplies. There would be no animals to hunt for food. The men would have to carry everything they needed. The journey would test their courage and strength.

Peary's expedition left New York in July of 1908. The group made camp in the north of Canada, on Ellesmere Island in the Arctic Ocean. The expedition left this camp on March 1, 1909. Peary had several **assistants**. Matthew Henson was one of them. Each assistant led a team of several **Inuit** men. Traveling on dog **sledges**, they took turns cutting a trail and moving supplies ahead. Peary planned to take just one team all the way to the pole. As the entire group grew closer to its goal, Peary sent the teams back, one by one. Fewer people meant he needed fewer supplies. As the returning teams headed south, they also kept the trail open. The open trail would help Peary find his way back. Otherwise, wind and ice would erase their tracks.

On March 31, 1909, Peary decided which team members would go all the way to the North Pole with him. He chose Matthew Henson and four Inuit men named Egingwah, Seegloo, Ootah, and Ooqueah. Of all Peary's assistants, Henson had the most experience in the Arctic. He spoke the Inuit language better than the others. He was also very good at sledge driving and dog handling.

Between March and April of 1909, Peary and Henson traveled from Ellesmere Island to the North Pole and back.

For five days, Peary, Henson, and the others struggled across the ice. They faced terrible cold, with temperatures below −50°F (−45°C). They traveled for ten hours at a time. Along the way, Henson and the Inuit men built igloos where they could sleep. The team grew thirsty because they did not have enough water to drink. For the little water they had, the men melted snow using portable stoves. They also used the stoves to dry their mittens so they would not get **frostbite**.

Henson often had to help the dogs by pushing the sledges over jagged piles of ice. Every morning, Peary would first start out on foot and travel for a few miles.

Henson and Peary used dog sledges similar to these from an 1875 expedition.

These are Peary's tools from his 1909 expedition (clockwise from lower left): a chronometer to tell time, an artificial horizon and mercury bottles used to find the horizon when ice blocked Peary's view, and a sextant.

This would be the route the team would drive a few hours later. Henson would soon catch up on his dog sledge. For the rest of the day, Peary then rode on a sledge driven by one of the Inuit. He was not as strong as he once had been. He had suffered frostbite many years before and had lost nine of his toes.

At last, the group reached their farthest point north on April 6. The team rested at their final camp. Peary estimated how far they had traveled. He used his **sextant** to determine the sun's location. This told him where they were. He calculated that they had reached the North Pole! They raised flags and posed for photographs. Then they loaded up their sledges and prepared to travel the 500 miles (805 km) back to their ship, the *Roosevelt*.

On April 3, Henson had an accident. As he crossed moving ice, he fell into frigid water. He was lucky. Ootah reached him and grabbed him by the back of his neck, saving Henson's life.

Henson on the deck of the expedition ship, 1908-1909

Chapter Two

YOUNG MATTHEW HENSON

atthew Alexander Henson was born on August 8, 1866. The Henson family lived in Charles County, Maryland. Matthew's parents were different from most other black people who lived in Maryland at the time because they had been born free.

Matthew's mother died when he was young. His father died only a few years later. After the deaths of his parents, Matthew either lived with his stepmother or with an uncle. Matthew stopped attending school when he was fairly young to work as a dishwasher.

At the age of 13, Matthew met a sailor. The man told wonderful stories about his trips.

Matthew decided that he wanted to be a sailor and see the world. A few days later, he walked 40 miles (65 km) to Baltimore, Maryland.

Baltimore was an important port city. Matthew hoped he could find work on a ship. On the docks, he met a kind old man named Captain Childs. Childs sailed all over the world, stopping at ports to buy and sell goods. He told Matthew he could go along as a **cabin boy** on his next voyage.

Matthew worked with Childs for several years. Soon, he could hoist sails, tie knots, and read charts. Childs also taught him geography and history. By the time Matthew was 17 years old, he had sailed across the Atlantic and Pacific oceans, as well as several other seas.

Slavery was legal in Maryland until 1865. That year, the Northern states won the U.S. Civil War. The Thirteenth **Amendment** *to the U.S. Constitution ended slavery everywhere in the United States.*

Henson sailed on ships similar to this one, a nineteenth-century clipper ship.

In 1883, Captain Childs died while on a voyage. After the ship returned to port, Henson no longer went to sea. For the next several years, Henson took whatever work he could find. Around 1886, he moved back to Washington DC. He lived with his sister and her family and worked as a clerk at a clothing store. One day in 1887, Robert Peary entered the shop. Peary was a U.S. Navy **engineer**. He had just returned from a trip to the island of Greenland. He was ten years older than Henson.

The U.S. Navy had asked Peary to make a map of Nicaragua, a small country in Central America. Peary heard Henson talk about the time he had spent sailing the globe. Peary asked Henson to come along as his **valet**. Henson later wrote that he did not want to become a servant. But Peary was an unusual man. Henson believed Peary would treat him fairly.

In the late 1800s, people were interested in what was called the "Greenland problem." Northeast Greenland did not appear on maps because it had not yet been explored. Robert Peary had gone there because he wanted to be the one who discovered the exact shape of the island. He hoped exploring Greenland would make him famous.

Robert Peary, shown in a late nineteenth-century photograph

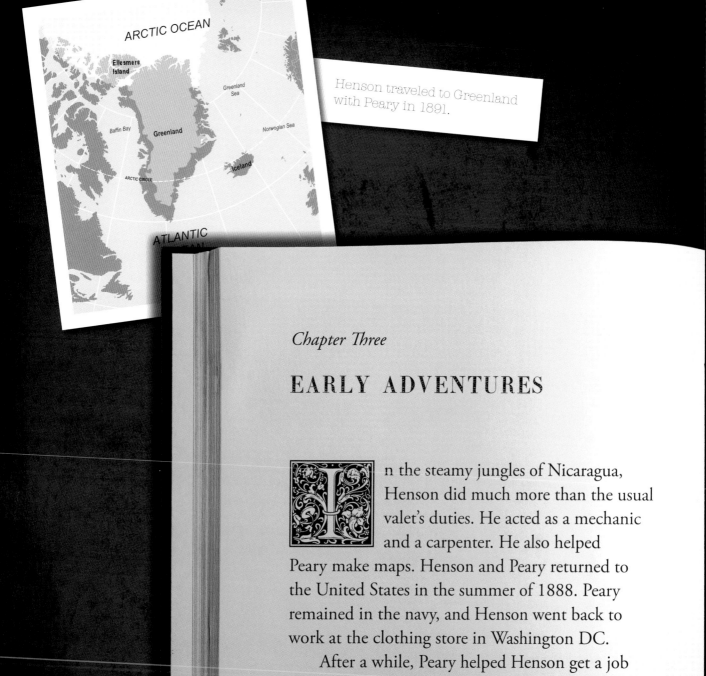

Henson traveled to Greenland with Peary in 1891.

Chapter Three

EARLY ADVENTURES

In the steamy jungles of Nicaragua, Henson did much more than the usual valet's duties. He acted as a mechanic and a carpenter. He also helped Peary make maps. Henson and Peary returned to the United States in the summer of 1888. Peary remained in the navy, and Henson went back to work at the clothing store in Washington DC.

After a while, Peary helped Henson get a job as a messenger at the League Island Navy Yard in Philadelphia, Pennsylvania. For a time, Henson felt like an outsider in the new city. However, he soon began to make friends. He met a young woman named Eva Helen Flint. Before long, Matthew and Eva talked of marriage.

In February of 1891, Peary told Henson that the U.S. Navy had agreed to give him time off for his expedition to Greenland. Peary asked Henson to come along as his personal assistant. Henson would have to quit his job to make the journey. Eva did not like this. But Henson told her he hoped the trip would gain fame for both Peary and himself. It was a difficult decision, but Henson accepted Peary's offer. Eva agreed with the plan. On April 16, 1891, Henson and Eva married.

Peary meets with Inuit members onboard his ship and gives them gifts.

In June, Peary began his second trip to Greenland. Four other men and Peary's wife, Josephine, went with him and Henson. On board their ship, the *Kite*, Henson organized the team's supplies.

On July 26, the group went ashore. Henson built a shelter where the group spent the winter. During this time, Henson began to meet Inuit people. (Like others who traveled to the Arctic in those days, Henson and Peary called these **natives** Eskimos.) Henson became friends with the Inuit. He learned to speak their language and taught them some English. The Inuit invited Henson to hunt with them. They taught him how to drive the dog sledges they used to travel over snow and ice. They showed Henson how to build igloos, and they gave him warm clothing made of fur.

In the spring of 1892, Peary and his men set off to cross Greenland. Peary's wife stayed behind in the camp. The trip was very difficult. Henson had to turn back early. He was disappointed, but he still felt happy that he had made the journey to the Arctic.

This was the first of seven trips to the Arctic that Henson would take with Peary during the next 18 years. They came close to starving on their 1895 expedition. Eva grew tired of Henson leaving home for long periods of time. They divorced in 1897. On the next expedition in 1898, Henson and Peary faced especially chilling cold. Frostbite caused Peary to lose nine toes.

Peary founded the Peary Arctic Club to help him reach the North Pole. The club raised money for the expedition. People began to read about Peary in newspapers. When Peary made speeches, Henson helped him. He even wore Inuit clothing at such events.

In 1901, they finished exploring Greenland's farthest reaches. Henson called it a "long race with death." When they returned home, Henson vowed never to return to the Arctic. Henson had learned to love life in the icy northern climate, however. Peary started making new plans. What he really wanted was to be the first person to reach the North Pole. Ultimately, Henson decided to join Peary in the adventure.

In 1905, Peary and Henson returned to the Arctic. They made it farther north than any exploring team had ever gone, but they had to turn back before reaching the North Pole. The group reached a point where the **polar ice cap** had broken, revealing the frigid water that lay below. They could walk no farther. They also ran out of food.

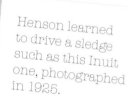

Henson learned to drive a sledge such as this Inuit one, photographed in 1925.

Peary and his expedition meet their relief crew in Greenland in 1892.

On their journey home, the men decided they would try to reach the North Pole once more the next year. Peary was 50 years old, and Henson was nearly 40. This would be their last chance.

By this time, Peary depended on Henson. A strong man, Henson worked well with his hands. He could make an igloo quickly. He built strong sledges, and he could fix them when something went wrong. Henson was a great outdoorsman, too. He hunted animals for food and used the furs to make warm clothing. He was also in charge of training the dogs that pulled their sledges.

Henson got to know the people who lived in the Arctic. The Inuit liked Peary because he gave them things in exchange for their help. But they saw Henson as a friend. The Inuit nicknamed him Maripaluk, *or "kind Matthew."*

17

Peary's ship, the *Roosevelt*, locked in Arctic ice

Chapter Four

TO THE NORTH POLE

pon returning to New York, Peary started raising money for the next expedition. Henson worked on their ship, the USS *Roosevelt*. He gathered supplies and equipment. He also married his second wife, Lucy Jane Ross.

Peary hired five other assistants for the expedition. He also hired a ship's crew. They sailed from New York City on July 6, 1908. President Theodore Roosevelt came to the harbor to wish them well.

By the first week of August, the *Roosevelt* reached Greenland. The ship docked in the northern village of Etah. Peary found several Inuit families to travel with them. The families brought along hundreds of dogs.

Henson, right, poses on a sledge onboard the *Roosevelt* with other expedition leaders.

Ice in the water made the journey slow and difficult. On September 5, 1908, the ship landed at Cape Sheridan, on Canada's Ellesmere Island. The explorers made a camp where they spent most of the next winter getting ready for their trip across the ice.

Henson went on several hunting trips, leaving camp for days at a time. Back at camp, he got the equipment and supplies ready. He built 24 sledges. He worked with the Inuit's dogs. All winter long, Henson and other members of Peary's team drove dog sledges farther north, leaving supplies the expedition would use on its trip to the North Pole.

On February 18, 1909, Henson and a group of Inuit left the *Roosevelt* for Cape Columbia, a point farther north on Ellesmere Island. That morning, the thermometer read –28°F (–33°C). It took four days to reach Cape Columbia. When the group arrived, they built what they called "Crane City," a camp with several large igloos. From Crane City, they would move supplies to Cape Aldrich. From there, Peary planned to leave land and move out onto the frozen ice.

On February 28, Peary sent team member Robert Bartlett ahead of the others. Bartlett and three Inuit would make a trail for the others to follow. On March 1, Peary ordered the rest of the group to follow.

Henson and the others went for three months without seeing the sun. In the winter, the sun never rises in the Arctic. The temperature can dip to –60°F (–51° C) or colder. The strong winds can blow heavy objects through the air.

The expedition's northern Greenland camp, 1909

Peary had calculated that they would have to travel 413 miles (665 km) to reach the North Pole. For the next month, each of Peary's teams took turns leading the way. The lead team created a trail and moved supplies forward for the rest of the group.

The trip across the frozen polar sea proved difficult. Sometimes the group had to use axes to cut paths through piles of ice. When sledges broke down, they had to stop to fix them. Henson would never forget the pain he felt when he had to remove his mittens in the biting cold to tighten the sledge straps.

Sometimes the men encountered extreme danger. They had to cross ice **floes** that could break off at any time. If this occurred, team members could have been stranded on a floe, unable to get back on land. The group once waited for almost a week to cross what they called the "Big **Lead**," an area where water ran freely between ice floes.

On March 14, Peary began sending teams back to the *Roosevelt*. Henson led the remaining teams forward. An hour later, he came to a small lead. He had to find a way to go around it. Their new route took them through snow so soft and deep that the sledges sank. Finally, the group made it through this difficult section.

But they immediately faced another challenge. Just ahead, they found jagged piles of ice. They had to use their axes to hack away some of the ice. Then they had to push it aside and clear a path.

On March 19, everyone made camp together. The next morning, Peary sent back assistant George Borup and his team of Inuit. Soon, the rest pushed on. On March 27, Peary sent back Ross Marvin and his team. On April 1, Robert Bartlett received orders to head back. Bartlett was unhappy at first because he wanted to continue to the North Pole. But Bartlett later admitted that Henson was a better sledge driver and could help Peary more than he could.

There were just six people left in the expedition: Peary, Henson, Ooqueah, Ootah, Egingwah, and Seegloo.

Expedition members get their dog team across a lead.

Henson wrote in his diary that the dogs became hard to handle as the group made its way north. Sometimes the dogs would do nothing, acting stubborn. Other times, they fought fiercely with each other.

Finally, on April 6, Peary decided they had reached their goal. He planted the American flag, and the group took photos.

Now it was time to head home. Peary had become so tired that he could no longer walk. He rode a sledge the entire way back. The men were all miserable during the return, but Henson felt little fear. He enjoyed the sunlight, which was getting brighter every day.

On April 23, 1909, Peary's group set foot on solid earth. They soon made it back to the *Roosevelt*. Henson said sad good-byes to his Inuit friends. Never again would he return to the Arctic.

For the rest of his life, Peary suffered from the injuries he received in the Arctic. The expedition had been very difficult for him. Henson had saved Peary's life at least twice, first when Peary nearly drowned and later when a **musk ox** attacked him. Henson was in better health than Peary at the end of the trip. Still, Henson had lost 60 pounds (27 kg) during the expedition and returned stressed and tired.

In 1910, Robert Peary wrote a book about the expedition to the North Pole. An entire page listed the awards and medals he had received. Matthew Henson received far less attention. Some newspaper stories mentioned him, but only in passing. The general public did not take notice of Peary's most important assistant, but many black people did. In the coming years, the black community would frequently honor Henson.

The expedition members raise flags at the North Pole on April 6, 1909. Henson stands at the center.

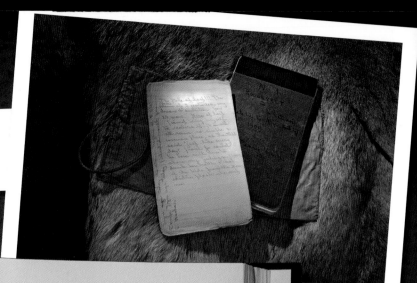

Robert Peary wrote daily notes from his North Pole expedition in this journal.

Chapter Five

AFTER THE POLE

hen the expedition members returned to New York, they received some bad news. Another man, Dr. Frederick Cook, had just claimed that he had reached the North Pole first! The controversy continued for years, but today most experts believe that Peary's group was the first to reach the pole. Later, Peary gained recognition as a hero. He received many awards. He published his story and gave lectures about his experiences.

Henson wrote his own book about his experiences, called *A Negro Explorer at the North Pole*. It was finished in 1912. For years, Matthew Henson's achievements went unnoticed by many people. However, Henson was better recognized

Peary brought this flag on the polar expedition.

in the black community. He lectured at black colleges. He was honored with degrees from Morgan State College and Howard University.

In 1937, the Explorers Club invited Henson to become a member. This club included only people who had undertaken serious voyages of exploration. This meant that other explorers voted to recognize Henson as an important explorer, too.

In 1947, writer Bradley Robinson published a book titled *Dark Companion*. Robinson based the book on interviews and conversations with Matthew Henson. Henson received many honors in his later years. In 1954, he was invited to the White House to meet President Dwight D. Eisenhower.

On March 9, 1955, Matthew Henson died at the age of 88. In 1961, the state of Maryland placed a plaque in its state house in his honor. Henson was the first black person to receive this honor. In 1988, Henson was reburied at Arlington National Cemetery with other national heroes, near Robert Peary's grave.

In 1945, like all the other American members of Peary's 1909 expedition, Henson received the U.S. Navy Medal. Unfortunately, because he was black, Henson was not invited to attend the ceremony where the others received their medals. Later, another ceremony was held to apologize for the injustice.

Henson meets with President Eisenhower at the White House in 1954.

S. Allen Counter, a black professor at Harvard University, became interested in Henson during the 1980s. He heard rumors that Henson had a grown son living in the Arctic. Counter traveled north to meet Henson's son by an Inuit woman. Counter brought Henson's Inuit relatives to the United States to meet the rest of Henson's family.

In recent years, some people have questioned whether the Peary party actually reached the North Pole. The National Geographic Society wanted to know the truth, so they asked the Navigation Foundation for help. This group of experts studies the science of navigation.

The foundation's experts performed many calculations. They carefully studied the notes in Peary's diary. They looked at the angle of the sunlight in his photographs. They performed other tests as well. The Navigation Foundation found reason to believe that Peary had indeed reached the North Pole.

Most experts now agree that Peary and his team reached the North Pole, or at least came very close to it. On this great journey, Matthew Henson earned his own place in history. He is remembered not only as an assistant to Peary, but also for his own amazing achievements during his years in the Arctic.

Courageous explorer Matthew Henson was the first black person to explore the Arctic.

TIME LINE

1860   1870   1880   1890

1866
Matthew Henson is born in Charles County, Maryland, on August 8.

1870
Henson lives with relatives after the deaths of his parents. He later leaves school to wash dishes at a restaurant.

1879
Henson goes to Baltimore and becomes a cabin boy on a ship headed for China.

1883
Henson gives up his life at sea following the death of his friend and employer, Captain Childs. Over the next several years, he holds a variety of jobs.

1887
As a clerk in a store in Washington DC, Henson waits on U.S. Navy officer Robert E. Peary. Peary hires Henson to accompany him as a valet on an expedition to Nicaragua.

1891
Henson marries Eva Helen Flint. Peary asks Henson to go with him on an expedition to Greenland.

1897
Henson and Eva get divorced.

1905
Peary and Henson try to reach the North Pole but fail.

1908
In the spring, Matthew Henson marries Lucy Jane Ross, his second wife. In July, Henson sails with Peary from New York City on a new expedition to the North Pole.

1909
The Peary expedition leaves their winter camp in Canada on March 1. On April 6, the team members reach the North Pole. They return to solid land on April 23.

1912
Henson publishes his autobiography, *A Negro Explorer at the North Pole*.

1936
After more than 25 years of working in modest jobs, Henson retires at age 70.

1937
The Explorers Club elects Henson to become a member.

1954
Henson is invited to the White House to meet President Eisenhower.

1955
Henson dies on March 9.

1988
Henson is reburied at Arlington National Cemetery.

Glossary

amendment
(*uh-**mend**-ment*)
An amendment is an addition or a change, including to the U.S. Constitution. The Thirteenth Amendment abolished slavery.

assistants
(*uh-**sis**-tentz*)
Assistants are helpers. Matthew Henson was Robert Peary's assistant.

cabin boy
(***kab**-in **boy***)
A cabin boy is a servant on board a ship. Usually, a cabin boy takes care of the needs of a ship's captain, such as doing his laundry and tidying up his cabin. Henson was a cabin boy when he was young.

engineer
(*en-jih-**neer***)
An engineer is a person who designs, builds, and takes care of engines, machines, roads, and other things. Robert Peary was an engineer in the U.S. Navy.

expedition
(*ek-spuh-**dish**-un*)
An expedition is a long journey made by one or more people for the purpose of discovery. Henson participated in an expedition to the North Pole.

floes
(***flohz***)
Floes are fields or sheets of floating ice. The Peary team had to travel across floes.

frostbite
(***frawst**-byt*)
Frostbite is an injury to a body part caused by freezing. In the worst cases of frostbite, a person may need to have part of the body, such as a finger or toe, removed by surgery. Peary lost nine toes to frostbite.

Inuit
(***in**-yoo-weht*)
An Inuit is a member of the native groups who live in Greenland and the Arctic regions of Canada and Alaska. In the past, the Inuit were often called Eskimos and some tribes are still called this today. Four Inuit reached the North Pole with Peary and Henson.

lead
(***leed***)
A lead is a split in the Arctic ice that exposes the water below. Crossing leads made travel in the Arctic difficult for the Peary team.

musk ox
(***musk ox***)
A musk ox is a native animal of Greenland that looks like a woolly ox. Henson saved Peary's life when he was attacked by a musk ox.

natives
(***nay**-tivz*)
Natives of a place are people who were born there. The Inuit are natives who lived in the Arctic before explorers and settlers arrived.

polar ice cap
(***poh**-lur **eyess kap***)
The mass of ice that covers the ocean at the North Pole. Henson traveled across the polar ice cap to reach the North Pole.

sextant
(***sek**-stent*)
A sextant is a special scientific instrument used to determine location. Years ago, sailors and explorers used a sextant to find out exactly where they were.

sledges
(***slej**-ez*)
Sledges are strong, heavy sleds. The Peary party traveled the Arctic on sledges pulled by dogs.

valet
(***val**-ay*)
A valet is a servant who takes care of a man's clothes and provides other personal care. Matthew Henson was once Robert Peary's valet.

Further Information

Books

Johnson, Dolores. *Onward: A Photobiography of African-American Polar Explorer Matthew Henson*. Washington, DC: National Geographic Children's Books, 2007.

Olmstead, Kathleen. *Matthew Henson*. New York: Sterling, 2008.

Sherman, Josepha. *Exploring The North Pole: The Story of Robert Edwin Peary and Matthew Henson*. Hockessin, DE: Mitchell Lane Publishers, 2005.

Videos

Glory and Honor. Dir. Kevin Hooks. Perf. Delroy Lindo, Henry Czerny. VHS. TNT, 1999.

Great North: Celebrating Man, Animal, and Landscape at the Top of the Globe. Dir. William Reeves. DVD. Slingshot, 2001.

Web Sites

Visit our Web page for links about Matthew Henson:

http://www.childsworld.com/links

NOTE TO PARENTS, TEACHERS, AND LIBRARIANS: We routinely verify our Web links to make sure they are safe, active sites—so encourage your readers to check them out!

Index